My First Book about the Alphabet of Insects

Amazing Animal Books Children's Picture Books

By Molly Davidson

Mendon Cottage Books

JD-Biz Publishing

Read More Amazing Animal Books

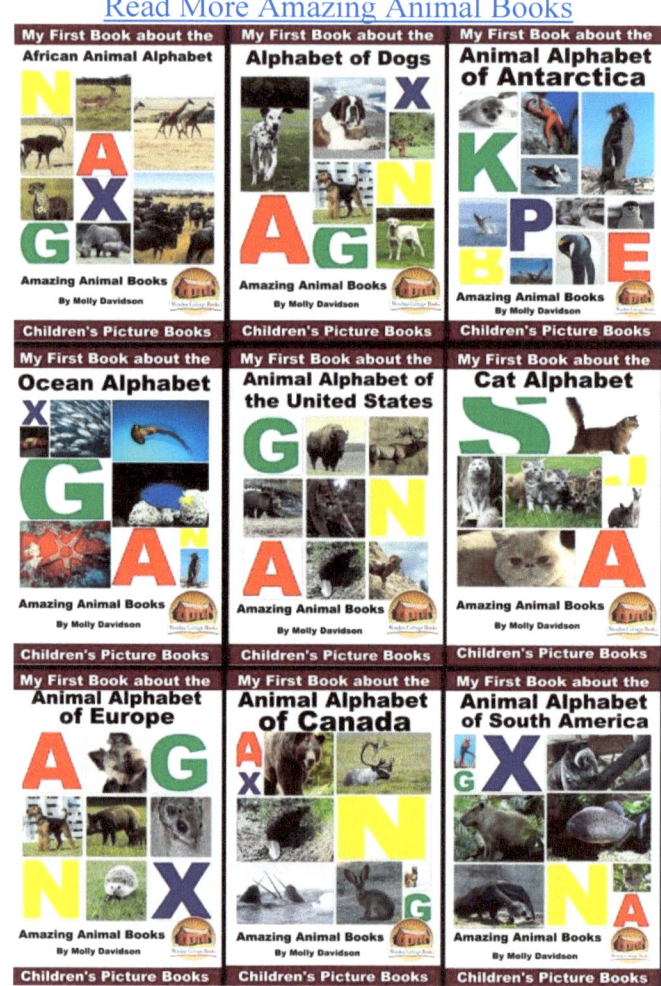

Purchase at Amazon.com

Download Free Books!

http://MendonCottageBooks.com

Introduction

Insects all have 6 legs and three body segments, a head, thorax, and abdomen.

Two thirds of all living organisms are insects!

Of all the insect species, 40% of them are a type of beetle.

 is for an Ant.

Ants live in large groups, called colonies, of thousands of ants.

They can lift up to 50 times their body weight, which is like a human lifting an elephant!

 is for a Black Swallowtail Caterpillar.

They are also called parsley worms, because they survive by eating parsley.

Their bodies produce toxins that taste gross to predators when they try to eat them.

These caterpillars and the butterflies they turn into, like tropical and warmer weather.

C is for a Cicada.

The word cicada means "tree cricket," because of the loud noises they make.

They do not walk very well, but they are excellent jumpers and fliers.

Cicadas drink tree and plant sap.

D is for a Dragonfly.

Dragonflies live around swamps and lakes; this is also where they lay their eggs.

They only eat meat, flies, mosquitoes, bees, and other small insects.

 **is for an Earwig.**

Earwigs are the smallest insect found on Earth.

They have wings that they keep hidden; they rarely ever fly, even though they can.

Girls lay about 80 eggs at a time, which take only a few weeks to hatch.

 **is for a Firefly.**

Fireflies, also called lightning bugs, use their glowing abdomen to talk to each other and to attract a mate.

They like to live in warm, humid, and tropical areas all over the World.

G is for a Grasshopper.

Grasshoppers get their name due to the fact that they live in warm, grassy meadows, and they use their powerful back legs to jump around.

Girls lay their eggs in the fall, and the babies, called nymphs, will not hatch until it is warm in the spring.

 **is for a Honey Bee.**

Honey bees live in hives of up to 40,000 bees, in the summer.

They are actually endangered due to humans taking over their habitats.

One third of all the food humans eat is pollinated by honey bees!

I is for an Inchworm.

Inchworms aren't actually a worm; they are a caterpillar which will one day turn into a geometer moth.

Some inchworms spin silk, like a spider, and will hang from it when predators approach.

 **is for a Junebug.**

The Junebug, or May beetle, lives in the North East United States and South East Canada.

They lay their eggs deep in the soil, where the larvae live for 2 - 3 years eating roots of plants, and then they come out of the ground as a beetle in the spring.

 **is for a Kissing Bug.**

Conenose bugs, nicknamed the kissing bug because they suck blood from the face of their dead prey, eat raccoons, opossums, and wood rats.

They grow to be between 14 - 24 mm long.

L is for a Ladybug.

Ladybugs are very helpful to gardeners and farmers, because they eat tiny plant destroying bugs called aphids.

Girls can lay up to 2,000 tiny yellow eggs per year, and they only take a few days to hatch.

M is for a Mosquito.

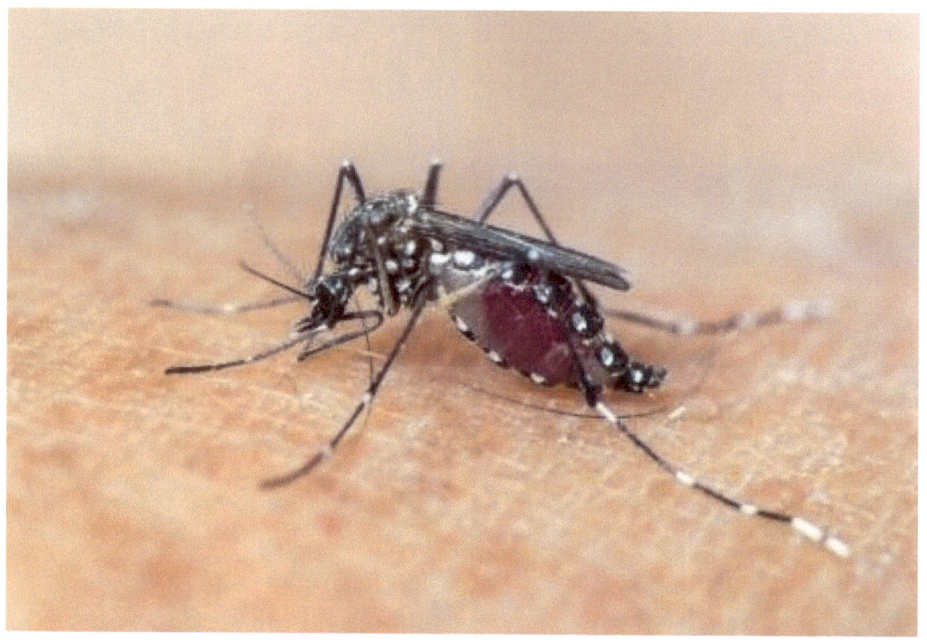

Mosquitoes are the deadliest animals on the planet, due to all the diseases they carry.

Only when the girls are laying eggs they feed on blood to get protein for their eggs, the boys just eat plant nectar.

 **is for Night Crawlers.**

Night crawlers live deep in the soil during the day, and come out to eat dead leaves and grass during the night.

They have between 8 - 10 babies per year, and can live for up to 10 years.

O is for an Owlfly.

Owlflies look like dragonflies, but they are different, one main difference is an owlfly will rest their wings on their antennae, not on their body.

They live mostly in the tropics and the southern United States.

P is for a Praying Mantis.

They are another helpful insect to gardeners and farmers, because they eat many crop destroying pests.

They are easily camouflaged, since they look like a branch or leaf.

Q is for a Queen Alexandra's Birdwing Butterfly.

Queen Alexandra's Birdwings are the largest butterflies in the World, spanning up to 25 cm (10 inches).

 **R** **is for a Robber Fly.**

Robber flies stab their prey will their sharp beak, and inject them with toxins that turn their insides to liquid, so then they can suck it out.

They are mostly found in Thailand.

S is for a Stink Bug.

Stink bugs have glands in their abdomen that will release a horrible scent when they are threatened.

They are known to eat and destroy farmers' crops, like soybeans in Japan, and juicy fruit and vegetables in the United States.

T

is for a Termite.

Termites live in large colonies, of up to several million.

They eat dead wood, plants, and soil.

Termites are eaten several places throughout the World, because they are a good source of fat and protein.

U is for an Unlined Giant Chafer.

Didier Descouens © <u>Wikimedia Commons</u>

The unlined giant chafer is a type of beetle found in North and Central America, Asia, Africa, and Europe.

They live in forests and orchards, where they lay their eggs in the soil.

 **is for a Viceroy Butterfly.**

The viceroy butterfly lives in the forests of the northern United States and southern Canada in the summer, and then they migrate in the thousands to Mexico for the winter.

They mimic, or copy, the Monarch butterfly as a form of self defense.

W  is for a Water Skitter.

Water skitters spread their weight evenly on their six legs and two antennae, which is how they can stay on the top of the water.

They bounce on prey that falls onto the water.

They fly to a warmer climate, out of the water, during the winter.

 **is for a Xylodromus.**

Udo Schmidt © Wikimedia Commons

The xylodromus is part of the stapylinidae beetle family, the largest beetle family with over 63,000 different species!

They live mostly under the bark of dead trees.

 **is for a Yellow Jacket.**

Yellow jackets are a type of wasp, whom doesn't lose their stingers after stinging.

Some live in nests of up to 100,000 yellow jackets.

Z is for a Zimmerman Pine Moth.

The larvae of Zimmerman pine moths burrow into the trunks of trees, causing many problems, like branches dying and breaking off.

They can be found mostly living east of the Rocky Mountains in the United States.

Conclusion

We hope you have enjoyed learning about insects, and to end we have one more fact.

Insects are found all over the World, by the millions, except in Antarctica, there is only one known insect, the wingless midge.

tasteofcrayons © <u>Wikimedia Commons</u>

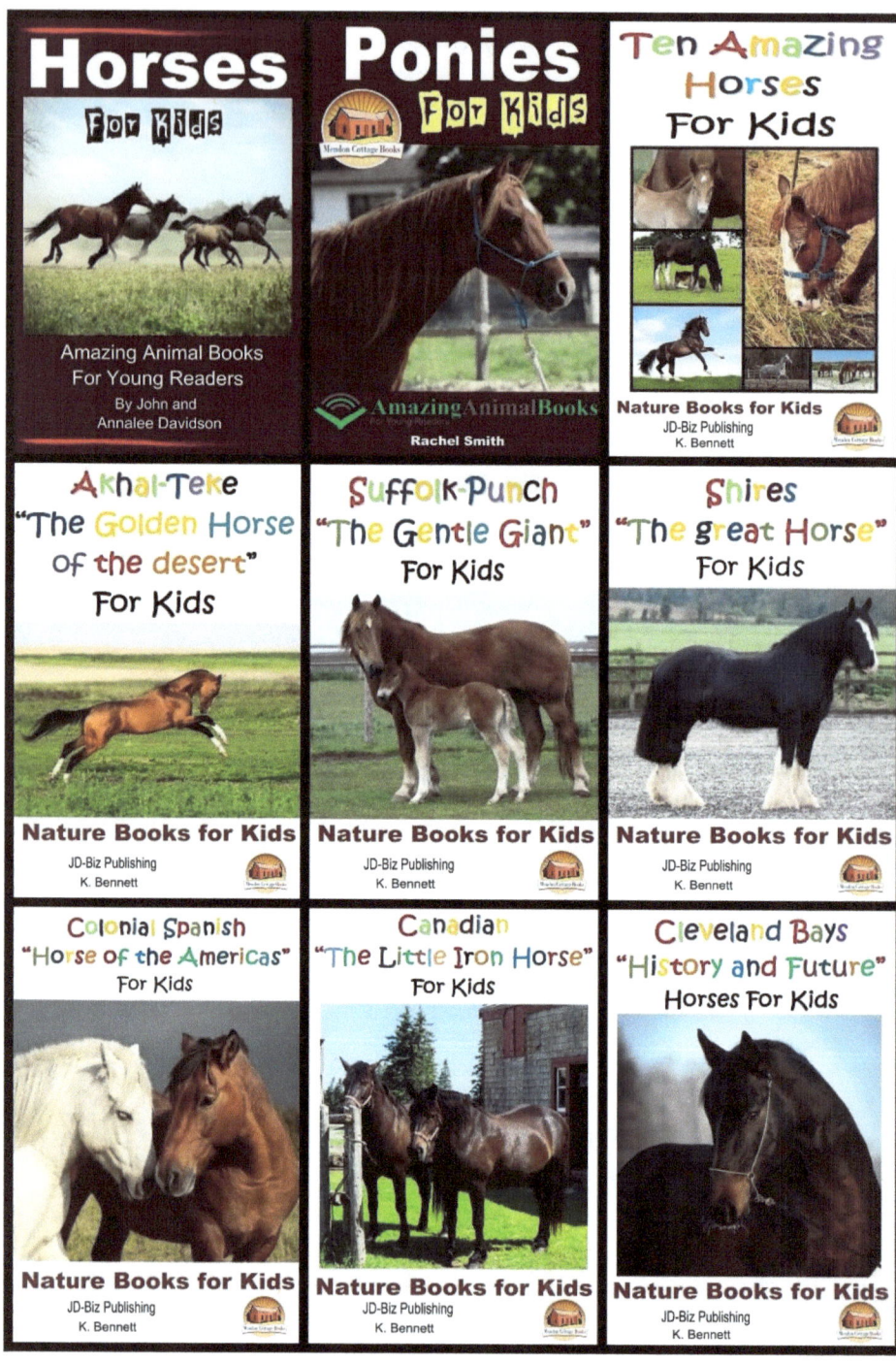

Our books are available at

1. Amazon.com

2. Barnes and Noble

3. Itunes

4. Kobo

5. Smashwords

6. Google Play Books

Download Free Books!
http://MendonCottageBooks.com

Publisher

JD-Biz Corp

P O Box 374

Mendon, Utah 84325

http://www.jd-biz.com/

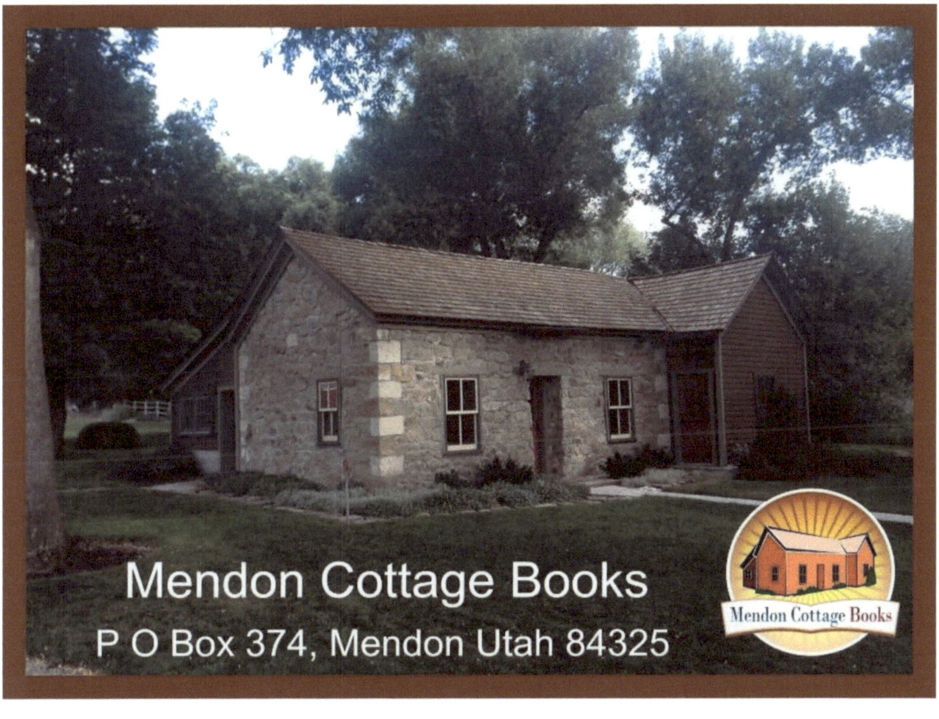

Mendon Cottage Books

P O Box 374, Mendon Utah 84325

www.ingramcontent.com/pod-product-compliance
Lightning Source LLC
Chambersburg PA
CBHW050902290526
45792CB00002B/672